Onyx Moon

Onyx Moon is the recipient of the 2018 William Meredith Foundation Award for Poetry. The Foundation was established in memory of poet William Meredith. As part of his long and distinguished career, from 1978 to 1980 Meredith was Consultant in Poetry to the Library of Congress, the position which in 1985 became the post of Poet Laureate of the United States of America.

Onyx Moon

Poems by J. H. Beall

Washington, DC

Copyright © 2018 J. H. Beall

New Academia Publishing 2018

All rights reserved. No part of this book may be reproduced or transmitted in any form or by any means, electronic or mechanical, including photocopying, recording, or by any information storage and retrieval system.

Printed in the United States of America

Library of Congress Control Number: 2017961129
ISBN 978-0-9995572-2-8 paperback (alk. paper)

 An imprint of New Academia Publishing

 New Academia Publishing
4401-A Connecticut Avenue NW #236, Washington DC 20008
info@newacademia.com - www.newacademia.com

The cover image of the 2017 Solar Eclipse is courtesy of pixabay.com (https://pixabay.com/en/solar=eclipse=sun-moon-astronomy-1116853). The author gratefully acknowledges its presence in the public domain, and notes that a solar eclipse is the ultimate Onyx Moon.

for MRC

Contents

Note on the title ... ix
Acknowledgments ... xi
Introduction: Star Light, Star Bright
  by Richard Harteis ... xii

Part 1 ... 1

Cicada ... 3
Millennium ... 4
Chicago Visits November ... 5
The Dream of St. Peter ... 6
Eumenides ... 7
Eye of the Storm ... 8
Gambit ... 13
The Gift ... 14
—for AJB ... 15
To Derrida, Opining ... 16
The Warmth of Clouds ... 17
White Carnations ... 18

Part 2 ... 19

Surety for Crito ... 21
On Gravity and Sorrow ... 22
After "My Books" ... 23
—for John ... 24
Icarus and Apollo Become Friends ... 25
Military Intelligence ... 26
911 ... 31

The Fire on Magdalena Mountain	32
Phoenix	35
Lucifer as a Work of Light	36
Odeon	37
Part 3	39
Memoriam	41
The Minstrel Show	42
The Moon Beside Antares	43
The Moth's Shadow	44
Pavane	45
The Portrait of Adam and Eve	48
After the Second War	49
The Thinghood of Monuments	50
Thinking of Picasso	51
Star-Crossed	52
Starlings	53
Red-Winged Blackbird at Gettysburg Field	54
Onyx Moon	59
The Moirae (or Parcae)	60
The Convergence of Meridians	61
About the Author	67

Note on the title, Onyx Moon: a Blue Moon is the second Full Moon in a calendar month. Likewise, a "Black Moon" or "Onyx Moon" is the second New Moon in a calendar month. The title poem of this collection, "Onyx Moon," was nominated for the Pushcart Prize in 2016.

t s beall: still from the video projection piece, "Here There Be Dragons," in the permanent collection of the Colby Museum.

Acknowledgments

Several of the poems in Onyx Moon have been published previously in Beltway Poetry Quarterly, Mipoesias, the Best American Poetry 2017, and others. This collection of poems owes a great debt to friends who, through their kindness and encouragement, have nudged me ever so gently to publish it. I thank my colleagues at Toad Hall Press and the Word Works, and especially Maria van Beuren, Karren Alenier, Nancy White, Laura Orem, and most especially Grace Cavalieri for their continued support. I also owe a special debt of gratitude to Richard Harteis, head of the William Meredith Poetry Foundation, for considering this book worthy of the 2018 William Meredith Foundation Award for Poetry.

As always, thanks to Mary, Tara, Aaron, Kelly, and Emma for showing me where true north really is.

t s beall: still from the video projection piece, "Here There Be Dragons."

STAR LIGHT, STAR BRIGHT
The poetry of James Beall

If there were ever an ideal candidate for the the 2018 William Meredith Award for Poetry, James Beall is close to the top of the list. First off, his new collection of poetry, *Onyx Moon* is such an exquisite work, poems from a master poet like Meredith, whose classical background and artistic talent combined with a scientist's curiosity and attention to the details of the wide world match those of his friend and colleague William Meredith. Wind, rain, volcanoes, jungles, mountains, and always stars weave their way through his poems, and like Audubon he paints his subjects with exactitude of color and precision of detail.

A working association with Meredith is not a pre-requisite for awardees, but in Jim Beall's case, their history as colleagues in the art makes an even stronger case for this award which the William Meredith Foundation is honored to present as the 2018 Award for Poetry.

In 1978, Beall approached William at a poetry reading at the Folger Library while Jim was a Congressional Science Fellow at the Office of Technology Assessment for the U.S. Congress. As the US Poet Laureate, the Library of Congress had approached Meredith about putting together a symposium on science and literature which led to an invitation by Meredith to visit him in the Poetry Office. Their collaboration led to The Science and Literature Symposium in 1981, with Beall as co-moderator. The program featured lectures by the the Nobel Laureate in Chemistry, George Wald, O.B. Hardison (then director of the Folger Library), Sir Fred Hoyle, Gerry Pournelle, and Gene Roddenberry of Star Trek fame, among many others.

Stars shine brilliantly throughout *Onyx Moon* as one would expect from a physicist. In his poem, "The Fire on Magdalena Mountain," he recounts travel to the large array of radio telescopes near Soccoro, New Mexico:

They are like flowers tracking a dark sun.
Those distant instruments listen to the sibilant
stars, stars that mimic no human speech. It is a sound
similar to the wind blowing across old ruins,
a level just beneath hearing, that conjures
beyond our capacity to understand or comprehend.

But like the camouflage worked into the coat of a stray buck who crosses their path, "mottled with the color of pine bark and rock," the poet intuits, "a sort of randomness, a kind of plan." One thinks of the "bright watchers" in Meredith's poem, "Country Stars" comforting the near-sighted child on a winter's eve, to have no fear, or "only proper fear," as elsewhere in Beall's poem, "Pavane," the poet lassos the stars with similar lyric beauty and ambiguity:

Then will be silence and a beauty there
upon the snow: a thousand crystals drear
and cold, refracting pale light, the sun
late in the winter slant walking

its rainbow speckles upon a frozen sea
crafted by storm and left so we may wonder
at the wasted, dormant time, where yet
the cold night comes and with it
other wastes of stars.

James Beall's work is at first an enigma. What to make of his challenging vision, his unique voice, the round-about syntax, his penchant for unfamiliar diction, his seemingly schizophrenic take on the world. For here is a poet blessed with double vision, a man who sees the world with both brain and heart, who is fully at home in his bicameral mind, scientist and mystic at once.

The literary landscape is rife with physician poets, of course. Poetry has long been linked to medicine; in mythology, the Greek god Apollo was responsible for, among other things, both healing and poetry. Poets like John Keats, Oliver Wendell Holmes Sr. and William Carlos Williams were all trained as doctors. One thinks of the late poet, Dannie Abse who wore both "white coat and purple coat."

But fewer poets who are also physicists come to mind unless one considers Einstein whose theory or relativity reputedly came to him in a dream, or the kinship between theology and quantum physics found in the work of John Polkinghorne who is both a theoretical physicist and Anglican priest. One thinks of the Jesuit scientist Teilhard de Chardin who posits that even the very rocks have a kind of living energy or "rayon" which is accumulating into an omega point from which mankind is about to make an evolutionary leap. It is not an exaggeration to find the same sort of philosophical insight in Beall's poetry.

Here we see both the careful scientific method of observation leading to a thesis as well as the appreciation of synchronicity that informs the reality of a Reike practitioner or a shaman. The two chevrons, orange-red on a blackbird's wings at Gettysburg mirror the late sun, the way the speeches of Pericles or Lincoln help his imaginary listeners understand a cause. In "Military Intelligence," soldiers digging a foxhole "will make of his or her small space/ a home of sorts, as carefully in place/ as any nest or den the animals/ or insects in their pantomime of thought,/ would take as ease." The soldiers here imitate the creatures around them as do the creatures imitating thought.

Often in Beall's poetry, a poem traces the poet observing his own thought process like a poem by the late John Ashbury. But in Beall's case, the poem is more accessible, more, frankly, "beautiful." The poetry constantly goes beyond the surface with a kind of x-ray vision. He is as interested in the shadows a moth creates, for example, as the creature itself:

"The sun swept on. The small window of shadow opened out./ As if it knew, the moth shook and shivered, warning/ the reedy center, prepared to fly." Walking the fields of Gettysburg, the scientist "... lingers to read the gentle lines the land/ makes, caused somehow by the layers of rock/ below these peaceful fields."

In a short poem memorializing 911, "the shiny pastures of his thought" could not finally befriend nightmare. Only after he describes the explosions with extraordinary metaphor, " the lesser suns/ began to blossom and bloom, before falling into darkness" can he afford the almost biblical summary at the poem's end: "Thus, the Angel of Mercy, made Fury again."

The final stanza of the final poem in the collection, "The Convergence of Meridians," mirrors the idealist philosophy of Ekhardt Tolle in his remarkable book, *The Power of Now:*

> There is a moment when all the past
> and future come together in the timeless now,
> a place with no part showing save the heart.

In 2015, astronauts and Star Trek actors performed the Vulcan salute upon the death of Leonard Nimoy. James Beall is no Pollyanna, but *Onyx Moon* is also a kind of greeting and blessing. As William Meredith writes in his poem, *The Cheer,* "Words addressing evil won't turn evil back, but they can give heart." James Beall too is one of the "bright watchers." *Onyx Moon* seems to say, as would Dr. Spock, "dif-tor heh smusma,": live long and prosper.

Richard Harteis
President, William Meredith Foundation

PART 1

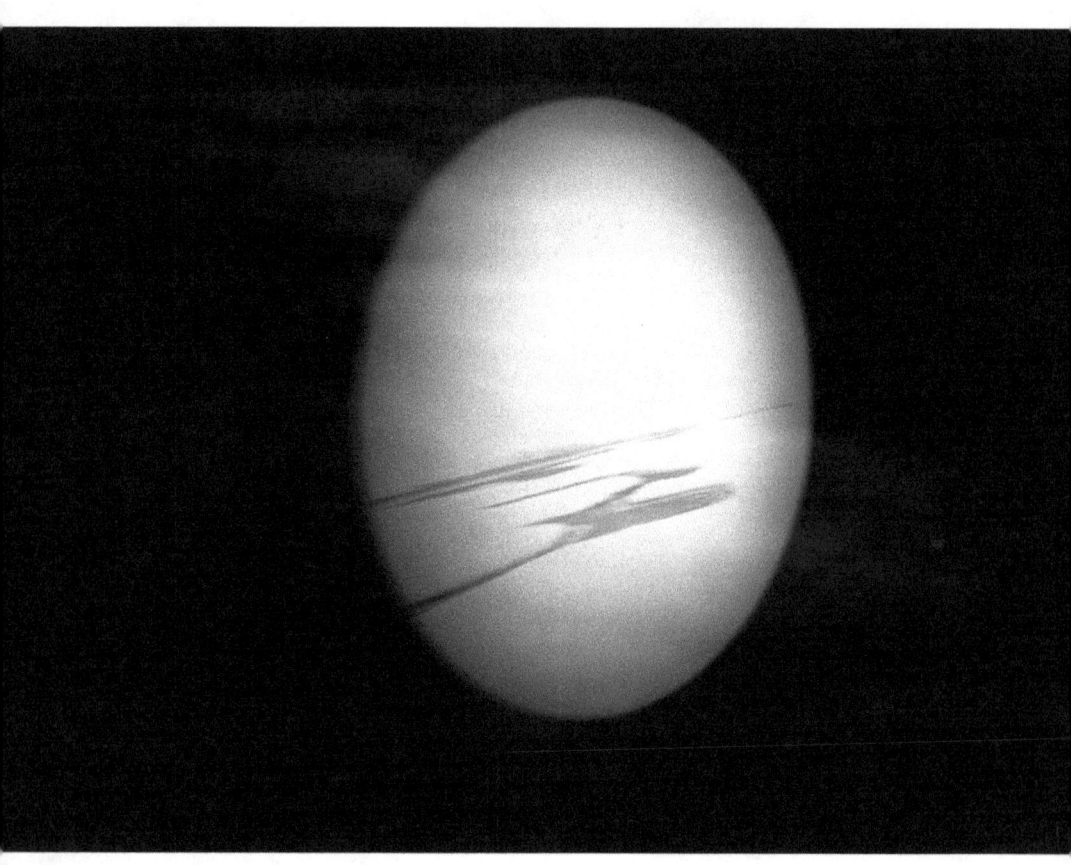

t s beall: still from the video projection piece, "Here There Be Dragons."

Cicada

Cicada, these the same
low boil into the building hiss
rising unto the jet's wail.
It the same, hence years will make

no difference. The heat encompassed
in its veil of air gathers us
like love's holding loose and slick.
Our bodies, then, are our bodies,

and love the metaphor for air.
But if insubstantial, still if fluid,
yet the holding forms a strange
and cyclic music, movements remnant

of a former self, used,
translucent, beneath trees.

Millennium

The way the tongues of flame gutter and sing
means the wood will burn a while. The cat knows
and shifts slowly from haunch to haunch
as though marking a rest upon a sunny ledge.

What will be left from this is a low fire:
orange coals and some blue jets of heat,
yet subtle as the shadow-shapes the logs
become on their way to transformation.

These will warm, still: the hand put up
as if to stay the cold, the hearth's back wall,
so like a cave. I watch as the first man might
have. In morning bless cold ash beneath my hand.

Chicago visits November

Not for long. The city rests there,
maybe a minute at a time. Then,
the sun comes out and we slide
into September, the warmer days.
Then the wind comes around a building
and the clouds come in. It is January, then.
The seasons slide up and down, fingered
by the weather into a great tune, chromatically
yellow to blue.

November's landscape changes like that.
First, you think it's early, then late.
Your senses forgive the mind's
delusioned equivalence of calender and state.
The season laughs, rolls its fat belly
in the process. The merry middle rolls by.
You think of every reason in summer
for the days to linger. Notice, finally,
the fading of the light.

The Dream of St. Peter

This is the dream: we are trying
to decide the soul of a man,
weigh its worth somehow to know
whether to open the gates and admit

him, weighed down like the rest of us
with his sorrows and joys, that strange
aura of light around the body sometimes
golden or perhaps gray — the color

of a particularly fine clay. Jesus
is always near but takes no part
at these times. He just crouches down,
his head bent, arm extended, finger touching

what passes for earth here. His position
reminds me of the time he was asked
to judge the harlot, how he crouched
down and wrote something

in the light, gray dust. Over and over
indecipherable letters are drawn. We all
ask what he wrote, but never where.

Eumenides

The old ones had a great wisdom about
the nature of retribution walking
on the human plane. How they called to them!
These "gentle sisters" who pursued Orestes

as he flew from their carnal shapes after the
righteous indignation at his act, blood
dripping from his mother's murderer's hand:
an act that seems to us no proper justice.

Yet in that light-drenched land, a grove filled
with a dense shade was set aside beneath
a shining city on the hill, to save us from
their terrible faces that live within us still.

Eye of the Storm

I.

Everything but the present moment is
expectation or memory. Consider this quiet,
autumnal air at late summer. The crickets
chirrup a lazy chime like a scythe at harvest.

The farmer's brown forearms, the dark stain
on his shirt, sweat, and its rivulets,
these are an expectation or memory
of another time and a time to come.

II.

Utter stillness. Is this a calm, or the eye
of the storm? Everywhere we look around
this harbor, the boats' reflections quaver
at each breath. We live the blessings

of peace and prosperity, are appalled
at what they cost.

III.

She is ingenue, a not-quite child, leaning
her hip against the table, or on tiptoes,
noting the menu taped on the window.
Her arms and legs have that amazing golden

color of a child in summer, the hair like
ripe wheat, cut to drape the nape of her neck.

IV.

We dawdle over the last wine, talking
of politics and Armageddon. On the periphery
of my vision I note the girl's turning,
her shirt the color of sky, some blue writing,
darker, above her heart, above the buds of breasts.

V.

I turn my head to read what is written. Who in this age can say there are no revelations? That we are only the convergence
of accident and reflex? Here is what was written on the pale blue wall of memory:

Eye of the Storm.

Gambit
—after Gwen Howard's "A Game of Chess"

"The calm of gods above a troubled field"
takes each within their thoughts as hours pass.
The cautious pawns go out to meet their selves,
headlong the horses charge to slice and swerve

like words well-crafted on a pristine page,
the writ of history carving its own way.
The gulf to memory from hope or fear
is vast. And expectations often go astray

in moments where a glance can shift the poles'
High Heaven and dethrone what gods decreed,
these dancing two in whirling thougths aloft,
hoped ready for conjunctions in the newer air.

The Gift

The pale evening offers up a stirring
 in the trees, but tranquil somehow,
an expectation that the night
will bring up stars out of the darkness

rising from the East. We cannot say
for sure what will become of it. Only
Prometheus, tied to that rock
with his innards being eaten out

by a black bird, knows the future.
This darkness that rises over us,
it is like his. And he pays our price
for the two gifts he gave us: fire,

as fine a light as Lucifer's longing,
and the other, an ignorance of the time
of our own reckoning, a knowledge that
he rightly thought we could not bear.

—for AJB

There is not much of my life
I can tell you. There exist
walls of circumspection, even
the walls built of respect

for your self, which is not
the same as mine. This is so,
although we share the same
dismay at the meanness of some,

their dimness that demands of us
a looking askance so we
can see through the dark,
harsh landscape, the diaspora

that the truly human has always
become. These outposts are
the faces of friends and family,
the pure precision of a well-timed block

or strike, the warm glow
of harbor lights as refuge
from a sea with no horizon, only
wind-whipped waves and wildness towering.

To Derrida, Opining

No word from you has the power
of no word: the simple, equestrian mass
of a thought astride the silence, the brief
quiver along its flank the moment before

the explosion of movement, the instant
the spurs sink deep into the object
of our desire. Thus the web of the relative
present dissolves into an absolution,

the sins of our doubt becoming absolute,
the absolute of our knowing becoming thought.

The Warmth of Clouds

The warmth of clouds is in the mind
imposed upon them, not the glimpse
of chaos, but a curve of brow
so like a face, a rising up

from the water, whole, a form or shape
that somehow is of us, yet not ourselves.
So as these are, we are among the young,
who show themselves before us,

flitting dappled light. So, too, these
new before the world was tamed
when rising mist reveals what
word became its thought and light.

White Carnations
—for Leo Raditsa

The white carnations in a wide-mouthed jar
upon the table open from the green
criss-crossed stems. Beyond, the slattern
light seeps over shrub and window sill to mix

within the hues of white and green. The snow
becomes a landscape of its own, beyond,
belies the still life here, its mimic spring.
The snow, now falling soft as down, now pitched

across the yard like rendered dreams by wind,
comprises all. The world we made in speech
has come to memory, my present faith unequal
to the brink you stepped across.

PART 2

t s beall: still from "Terra Incognita."

Surety for Crito
—on an excavation of a house in Pompeii

The ash and dust are excavated, brush
by brush, to show the simple and pathetic
scene. Strangely, they lie, skeletal.
The walls have decoration. A domestic

view was here preserved in darkness through
a goodly age 'til we exposed the nakedness
of bone. They did not flee to be struck down
beyond their home, but stayed, somehow,

within the walls to be remembered here.
The only hint of their swift thoughts
is shown upon a floor in hieroglyphs.
The strange profusion in a gesture

of the remnant of a hand conjures a word
we would have lost had they more simply strayed.

On Gravity and Sorrow

I remember the feeling of my weight
upon you, your skin pressing back,
holding me against gravity and sorrow
that I knew even then would come.

There were the softest murmurs, your breath
coming quiet at first, then faster, the feel
of the tension's rise within you, its meeting
mine, then sinking to salt and to rest.

Now your eyes in memory move me. In memory
mine move across your breasts and belly
down to the cleft between us, this shame,
this distance, I can neither hold nor part.

After "My Books"

Even your title belies you. How could
you say your shapes are not your own?
Mewling that all this came from another,
from books, and in a poem, yet, a making,

you tell us this! Consider this the proof
against you: think of these words as hieroglyphs,
not even words, but marks, strange squiggles,
writhing in their too straight lines, their cages.

By themselves, they conjure nothing. Their lack of
speech is as silent as the murmurs of the dust between
the stars. It is as though from a vast distance
that we see them, mere shapes like those of the long

dead, who are but shades to us. And they remain
speechless, these twittering things, unless
like Odysseus, and all those others after him,
through you and me to the very present,

the reader give a living blood, so meanings rise
like mist and they become and thus speak true.

—for John

Because of the exigencies of your lives,
she did not know you on that street
in Prague with rain pouring from the sky
like cold tears on her face so many years ago,

except by a blink: the only motion
that might have kept each of you alive.
Nor did she say, later, among the poets
and in the soirees in the Capitol,

what you both knew: a particular sorrow that
each kept between you, a sort of life
In Praise of Secrecy, as though you moved
in other Circles. And to protect you, given

your station, she slit her lover's throat
and felt the other warm release after the first
within her, felt his will go slack, felt
his stiffness slacken, and the sorrow come.

Icarus and Apollo Become Friends

Meeting an old enemy is never easy: after
the threats and curses, after the knife blade
laid across his jugular simply because he was
in the other's country. At the small, round table

in warm summer sun at the Café du Paris,
in Vienna, Austria, the air should seem electric.
Yet for his part, the other seems a decent man. They talk
of their families, of the way the world is now:

changed utterly, still dangerous. With that, both of them
look askance, look around, realize with chuckles
that they are covering each other's backs. "Here's
to the New World." The only toast that seems fitting.

He is the classicist, of course. "To Icarus and Apollo,
becoming friends." How strange it is that sun and wine
will soften the hardest heart, as worked wax is softened,
during the mind's contemplation, by a persistent hand.

Military Intelligence
—for Clovis D. Ice
at Ice Hall, Ft. Jachuchuca, Arizona

I.

There is a drapery of mountains on
the line that sweeps on south toward a place
that some have called the other world, to Mexico.
Wind-etched by time and taut by acid tears

they frame the sedge of plains' wheat brown.
And contrasting, they complement somehow
both dust and sky. These are part of ages
and they know our comings on and leavings.

They will be watching as the night stirs
its lights, rounding the pole and pacing the dark,
with pale phosphors that comprise the Milky Way,
a glowing pigment smeared, entraining stars.

II.

The heat here does not touch the bone.
It waits, an insect song that hovers in the air,
like tan and dark-tan shadows in the trees
that mimic patterns that the soldiers wear.

Their sweat takes of its own dark stain, a bloom
in deepest stillness as they move across
scrub oak and scrabble to their destined lot:
Each for a night will make of his or her small space

a home of sort, as carefully in place
as any nest or den the animals
or insects in their pantomime of thought,
would take as ease. They mimic mottled light.

III.

Ice. That unlikely name, alone, suggests
a story and a song. I still recall
the bright, white light a Spring day cast upon
us, on his pale arms, and how we talked

of helping others when the words rounded
like a pack of hounds on one that hung in air:
Vietnam. An echo and a roadmap.
The image of a train, its hurtling

to an uknown station through a dark mist.
He was kind. I knew that. The light washed over us.
He talked of how he tried to help those others
make a better life. Two tours. No third.

"I don't think we are doing any good."
That was before we made our history
with blood. Before the dead grew on the banks
of Acheron to populate a good-sized city.

IV.

This low, flat building, and these pale trees
carve out some pools and flecks of shade. The thin and
silver leaves quake in scant breeze. Clouds build.
The bronze plaque at the entrance chronicles

but a brief story. A "soldier's soldier." The man
I knew. These inroads into the continent of euphemisms.
"National assets adopted to tactical use." The pioneer
I had heard some buildings somewhere had been named

for him. Here, the summer desert grows its buzzing
grasshoppers, its puffball, noontime clouds.
Later, the monsoon rains will come and lay their dark
tracks down. They make the desert bloom.

V.

Perhaps the strangest part is that we think
we know a life. We see an arc a flash
of movement as the lightning strikes, thunder
from a distant sway of cloud-wrought canyons.

Of gods or men, we cannot say. There was
the stutter and the slime of slow advance, raining
hard and darkness so we could not see the
tripwires, could not see ourselves or theirs.

Back in another place, the ones who stayed
within the "low flat buildings, unrelieved by time"
counted money and lives and years. Here, bitter part
of a brief run as the setting sun bleeds bronze.

911

We spoke as though the shiny pastures
of our thoughts could befriend nightmare.
It was an era of dumb-luck prosperity
after the last war that never is the last.

So when of a clear morning warmed
by the bright sun, the lesser suns
began to blossom and bloom, before
the falling into darkness, came

the recollection, "Ah! This my father
remembered, also too late. This my elder
brother gave to the dark way of the world."
Thus, the Angel of Mercy, made Fury, again.

The Fire on Magdalena Mountain

I.

In the mountains west of here, up
across the ragged country, the bare peak
takes its lightning straight, a pure
fire, like Tequila in the gut.

First, there is the leader's snick-snick,
then the wham of the strike like an old god's
thunder. The hatch of the Kiva is open slightly,
and those within instinctively jerk and laugh,

having survived the fire by a kind of daring
beyond my understanding or beneath the deepest
faith. They have tickled the dragon's tail,
for neither the first nor the last time.

II.

On the right day from this high vantage,
one can see far off to the west the giant
dishes, the radio telescopes of the VLA.
They are like flowers tracking a dark sun.

Those distant instruments listen to the sibilant
stars, stars that mimic no human speech. It is a sound
similar to the wind blowing across old ruins,
a level just beneath hearing, that conjures

beyond our capacity to understand or comprehend.
The opposite point of the compass in the broad sweep
so like a vision from some disparate and harried age,
holds a particular past called Trinity.

It is the place where we began a pilgrimage.
Was it a choice, a trajectory, or merely
chance that brought us to this moment so like
a pinnacle or a precipice in the high, thin air?

III.

The road to the peak is fretted, tacked
along the sides of the mountain. Here
and there, the haptic sense of space
squirms in the pit of the stomach.

Halfway up, a buck deer, his antlers high,
crosses the road, uphill to down, in front
of us. He steps with a kind of absolute
confidence off onto the impossible slope.

He takes the steps he must without
equivocation, clearly worried by
the oddly alien vision of the truck
grinding slowly, erratically, up the hill.

Then he's gone into the dense trees, his coat
mottled with the color of pine bark and rock,
a pattern honed by Darwinian forces, "The face
of nature hammered by a thousand blows,"

a sort of randomness, a kind of plan.

* VLA: the Very Large Array of radio telescopes near Soccoro, New Mexico.

Phoenix
—For Alejandro Vallega

Out of ashes rubbed into the forehead
as though a penitent for another's sorrow,
we hope for a kind resurrection: the dark
becoming a window, and the window light.

This, especially, after the flames of passion
or fortune consume the acrid weavings
of the past. Dawn, then, come blood-red
and singular, we awaken to the deep light

scattered down. From the thin air, smoke climbs
vine-like into memory, the tangle of jungle,
the volcanic sweep where whole trees explode
within the clasp of a bright river.

For this suffering, this question like Job's,
there is no answer. This far down even the silk
feel of loss rubbed between fingers, smudged
on the forehead, yields only the wet smell of dawn

at the gates of the East. We note the stirring.
What will become of this only the vast machines
of the will and the future can know.

Lucifer as a Work of Light

Francis Bacon in his cloister feverishly
works on his "Great Instauration," knowing
finally the subtlety of Nature and the
limitations of the human mind.

He lucidly sees the future laid out like a
great roadway or shining path where
light walks on the surface of water
toward a rising or a setting sun.

The "Idylls of the Tribe" are behind him.
He scribbles about the "Idylls of the Cave,"
of the need for Works of Fruit and Works
of Light that must come somehow from us.

He has the comfort of his theories, his
belief in a clear method. His words construct
a grand tower. We live in its shadow,
wondering why his Works of Fruit conjure

something like a Garden, why his Works of Light
bring to mind the Angel of Light, Lucifer.

Odeon

The mist within the trees lay lavender
an idyll that the dawn brought from the dark
as gifts are brought by supplicants to feast
where crazed and spinning dervishes of stars

trace out their patterns in transcendent arcs.
At times some spirit in the world can do
more than the million voices of a choir
to leach out sorrow from the ragged, stark,

and intersticed poles. By finger strokes
of warmth's originals, the skin will know
more than the thought can find by pondering
an evanescence in the wisps of snow.

PART 3

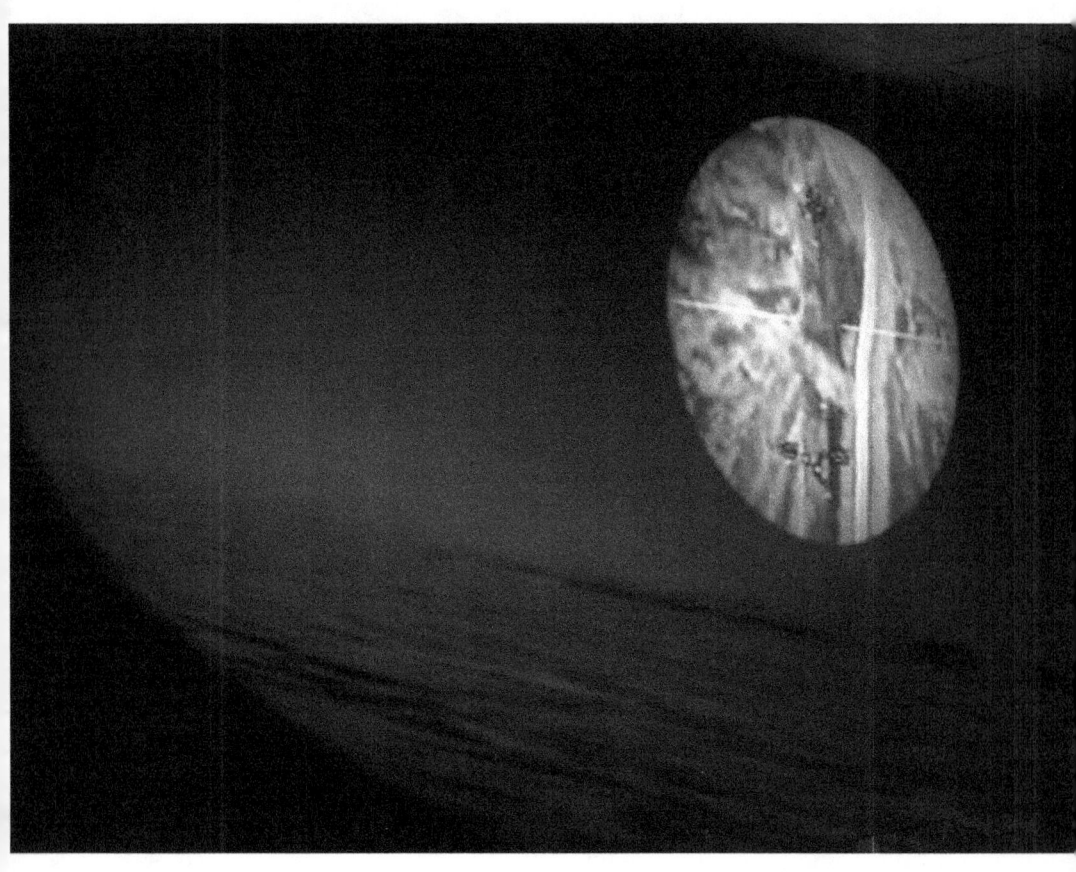

t s beall: still from "Endless War."

Memoriam

The day after you left was a day of raining
and the green intensity dotted by clovers
in patches which reminded me of foam
upon a wind-driven sea. Yet the air

was still, the gentleness of the rain
falling from a sky gray as the color
of lost memories or even of lost sight.
I do not know what I had hoped

would happen here upon this page,
itself a gray, a whiteness in half-light,
nor where you put the poems I gave you.
"A safe place," you said, but I cannot think
of where that would ever be.

The Minstrel Show
—for Tara

This day the wind spits wet against the window all
day of it into the darkening deep past noon, branches
mark the slow heave with tremulous fingers the leaves
remaining, like a dark minstrel show, palms aquiver.

I would have half expected a music come
dim, athwart the windows, of the singers there
waving their dark robes uncomprehendingly
to a slow, atonal music that lifts and lifts
like waves.

I think we do not see the whole of this, the branch
seeming to touch another, as the light goes into
its other self, $αλλοσ$, allele, $τὰ\ πάντα\ ῥεῖ$
somehow beyond understanding and beyond faith.

The Moon Beside Antares

The Moon low in its southern arc
full with a June and summer
fullness, with its light dwarfs
flinty Antares' orange sparks

and strikes the summer darkness
in counterpoint to cool fireflies'
light. So in the night
of fair beginning's season,

these metaphors that orbit
one another in a cosmic dance
hold court above the green
and august dark. Here

sprinklers scatter in their parabolic
paths the prayers of grasses:
glinting shards of light's laughter
from the Moon's missed mark.

The Moth's Shadow
—for Szczepan Karakula (1935–1996)

All day the wind struck tremulous chords or grand
upon the screen. Late afternoon the gilt sun gonged,
brassy, slant on fine mesh. Having survived the light,
the moth there cast the first discernible shadow of its
  wings.

They made a clear patch in the curious, confused bronze
  light.
The sun swept on. The small window of shadow opened
  out.
As if it knew, the moth shook and shivered, warming
its reedy center, prepared to fly. And yet another

bloomed and fell beyond, behind the trees,
at the vast lip of the world where the blood
of Homer laps its salt song upon a rocky shore.
Where, pale, the blue gives up to darkness

and the stars.

Pavane

I.

The cloud-capped world is separate
from its leaves, these scattered ochre
and brown. The few remaining in the trees
under a darkling sky that threatens rain

take on the luminous: the yellow and orange
of sunset, sunrise, the promise of resurrection
after the wiles of winter, its snow-topped
hedge, the marmot in his burrow, and puffed

and freezing on a bitter branch, a chickadee
chirping its seed-beak call that is not sorrow,
but lament. What of the human warmth
between us in this sweep will not be rent?

II.

This is an old companion, he who lurks up
in the low cloud-roll of the wind come
northeast and storm. There is a surcease
in the breaking, the knowing of fall

no longer waiting on its golden wing,
but strutting gladly back and forth,
fretting its lines out in a low moan
of winter in the wind around the house.

III.

Then will be silence and a beauty there
upon the snow: a thousand crystals drear
and cold, refracting pale light, the sun
late in the winter slant walking

its rainbow speckles upon a frozen sea
crafted by storm and left so we may wonder
at the wasted, dormant time, where yet
the cold night comes and with it

   other wastes of stars.

The Portrait of Adam and Eve

They are together in the picture you have
somewhere in your memory: he like David,
like Michelangelo's David, but before
the knowledge breaks upon him of who

he spoke to, a voice in a kind of Garden,
a knowledge of the Goliath the speaker
really was. She was ever more subtle,
and so was not too surprised when temptation

came in the form it always does, the form
of wanting to know. She was ready. Even
in the family portrait with its lucid
surface, there is that tension between them,

the expectation of hope on the one hand,
the recognition of sorrow on the other,
and the distance between them a force
like gravity that will not be denied.

After the Second War
—to M.E. Warren

I have seen the millennium as a dark shadow
arching above a boy lost in a fog. Yet he turns
toward the camera in a look askance as the shutter

snaps. Think of the photographer as predator,
waiting for days until the deer or antelope
come down into ambush—not the white-belly-bloodied,

the gaping maw, the soft tissue torn, then the cold.
But certainly, surprise, a recognition growing
as the light fades of its living moment held in thrall.

The Thinghood of Monuments

It is a city of spectacle, and I suppose
the best and worst of men have loved
these: the marble whiteness of gulls
whirling in the wind about a vacant
patch of earth that seems to contain
something to attract them,

or in the circumscription of the sky
clouded and chill above the back alleys'
apartments, a stirring that will yield
who knows what tomorrow — a beginning of
thoughts ready to form the indelible.

If we look at the thinghood of monuments
we might miss the feathery homage of bare
trees, branching to the sky. Yet I suppose
that the worst and best of men have loved
these: the Attic reach of columns, an occasional
building, seeming to be the edifice of power,

something after all dark and brooding
over an inhuman and inscrutable intent.

Thinking of Picasso

I.

What we make in walking here, the sea
will take, leaving no trace. Yet its peculiar,
urgent hunger, that is time itself, or a metaphor,
remains. It is, thus, not hunger that makes art, but desire.

II.

Mostly we notice the eyes of the man,
a kind of rapine intensity towards all that is seen,
as though something raged there. The works
show it, show that incredible need beyond tension
to make the lines work from charcoal and white paper
to volume, then, as though from dark clay,
to the living form oddly askew.

Star-Crossed

It was the love of the dark skies
that brought them together, that
silence beyond silences where
the great sphere, seeming, moves.

Who can imagine these vastnesses
between the separate stars, all unified
in the chaotic swirl of star-stuff,
the dark seeds of tomorrows' light,

entrained and mixed as though a hand
had moved it (or thought, or breath),
had stroked lightning inside a taut
thigh, the cool blue fire of starlight

playing within the wasted remnants of their
borning selves. So shed, the cloak,
we see this nakedness between them,
pure space, and warmth from new fires.

Starlings

The startling shadows flit or glide
among the trees. They are like absences
of light, a glossy black, their shapes
given to the cold you feel when you think

of distant stars and deeps unkenned.
Yet move they soft among the sun-struck
woods, that stand, rigid, against the cold,
even as their upper branches sway

to wind that comes from somewhere north.
No wonder that the minstrel branches show
a self-same movement as the dark, the world
is pitched twixt sky and what's below.

Red-Winged Blackbird at Gettysburg Field

I.

We linger to read the gentle lines the land
makes, caused somehow by the layers of rock
below these peaceful fields. We talk under
a copse of trees, mostly for shade from the sun.

A red-winged blackbird alights and bobs on distant
sedge, then launches itself toward the canopy
above us. Before it disappears, hurtling into
the fractured darkness of the trees,

its two chevrons, brilliant orange-red on black
wings, flash against the fractal blues and greens
of tree and sky. The wind shifts. The words
flutter to us of soldiers' battles and old wars.

II.

It is certain that these, red-winged, were here
in that time, when for three days — before
a kind of resurrection — the Fates gave Lee
his time to pose upon the stage of history.

Perhaps he saw them, bobbing and diving, crimson
chevrons showing before the cannons fired their first
volleys and they fled, these soldiers of the sky.
So, too, the soldiers of the earth, whose lives

were strewn about like litter, like false papers
rent from a kind of dark book not unlike history,
they too would have gladly turned to share
the sights of black birds and bright wings.

III.

In the beginning, there was the plan
the General thought out, so perfect in his mind,
a plan like a grammarian's composition. His will,
done in directing each element of his army.

Always, there is the unintended consequence.
The march of soldiers arriving too early
and too late. The desperate scrabble hand over
hand up the bloody hill into the face of an enemy

not unlike ourselves. And then the words seem
to become bidden, the terrible, gentle, words,
after the buried dead and the wailing, after the rain
sows ashes, wet and black, into the old earth.

IV.

Thus, the cause, these ideas, these shadows, spawn:
the orange ball of the setting sun which promises
a fair tomorrow, "red at night," red through
the dark clouds' gathering, red like the chevroned

wings which know nothing of thoughts, red
like the blood soaking into the fields from
the mindless dead. Still, we remember: brothers,
fathers, comrades, friends — the terrible, bloody

mark on his arm as the first bullet sang and slupped
through it, then the second, then the fall.

V.

We come to ponder, to feel the weight of leaden ages
which have brought us to this place. It is only natural
to speak of it, I suppose, to remember not the deeds
but the words. Pericles, whose speeches became

a city and an effigy of war. Lincoln, who gave us
his great equivocation upon a hallowed ground.
I see them, or the idea of them, with the wind tugging
at their clothes, the upturned faces longing

to understand a cause, as the late sun, shrouded,
becomes a crimson band upon a dark wing.

Onyx Moon

"He died east of here under an Onyx Moon"
in an older time. We have not seen his like
since. This is a letter from the Dark
Ages, of a place and time it is better

not to know. What is the wind coming to?
Or from? Which is the orb that rises north
of a convergence of tracks, dark rails
shining, seeming to have their own light.

We know in our minds these thin strings, barely
luminous, do not meet. But what does the mind
know, really? It is the heart that teaches us
dread. There is a mist in the sky in place

of stars. What compass can tell us, we
do not believe: the false convergence of tracks,
the true convergence of meridians, the pale
skin of a girl we knew once, becoming flame.

The Moirae (or Parcae)
—Clotho, Lachesis, and Atropos

The thunder mutters in the fading light
as green and lavender become the same
fell sky. The Moirae are at work
above in the dark wild, spinning out

the warp and woof of the great curtain,
measuring the tints of the first bright colors,
settling themselves – but especially Atropos
with her shears to cut the final thread.

Below the mariners pray to younger gods
as the dark bellows mount and the green
sea darkens into a glassy stone.
The web is ladled out with gossamer fingers,

as sailors cry to no good purpose, and the cold
mist rises, shrouds, encloses, and obscures.

The Convergence of Meridians

I.

The ache of this is the distance between
a warm, moist breath and a whisper,
the awful moment so much like
the coalescence of vapor into warm rain.

Who will recall that time when they stood
in the dread center, a place like some pole
that even the stars still have as they wheel
in turns and counter-turns? Now we live

in an age of parallels and asymptotes.
Lost to us, the careful convergence, meridians
that move off into a shrouded north
which hides what never can become.

II.

I woke last night late and walked
under the cold stars, the phosphor flecks
that harbor themselves sometimes
in the upper air with a closeness belied

by what I know: The Universe a vastness
incomprehensible as God was to Job.
Yet there is so much seeming silence here
with only the thoughts like whispers

lofting into the ineffable sky,
strangely pale and mostly dark.
This dark, this silence, caused
by the flinging away of remotest parts.

III.

After a while comes understanding
that the only asymptote, the single rail
which always approaches — which even though
it never touches can offer hope — that track

cannot be taken, that trajectory
cannot be walked. Here is the frozen
field at the end of things, here
the snow clearing and the sky give way

to a bottomless cold.   Here is
the bitterness of ages, the ruined temple,
canyons or crevices where the wind
whispers its dry song for no one's ears.

IV.

Who could believe in the coming cold?
No book and only phosphor the light
to read it by. What faith or patience
when the self, undone, is done?

Once there was a fiddler in a hall
whose strains of music caused a joy,
a veritable joy that seemed a dance
within the air, while far below

a wide-flung city burned to the clatter
of drunken boots, the thin echoes in a
temple hall.   Now the heart swells
with another tune as of meridians and latitudes.

V.

Suppose the perfectable: Let air
be light and light be love and love
be always there. Still there is
in the way of things the differential,

the same ratio, the infinitesimal
space that can evanesce or grow.
What if the path be taken?
What if the world be gone

before you are but memory? Still,
there is a moment when all the past
and future come together in the timeless now,
a place with no part showing save the heart.

About the Author

Jim Beall is an astrophysicist, a poet, and an author on issues related to public policy and national defense. He holds the degrees of B.A., M.S., and Ph.D, all in physics. He is a member of the faculty at St. John's College in Annapolis, Maryland, and a senior consultant to the U.S. Government. His first book, *Hickey, the Days*, was published in 1981 by the Word Works, Inc., and his second book, *Republic*, was published by Toad Hall Press in 2010. The Italian translation, *Repubblica*, translated by Sabine Pascarelli, was published by Toad Hall Press in 2013. *Onyx Moon* is his third book.

About the Artist

t s beall is a new-media artist based in Glasgow, UK, whose work explores how the camera and digital media have shifted our notions of place, and how landscape is both imaged and imagined by modern technology. She completed her Ph.D. at the University of Glasgow in 2017.

www.ingramcontent.com/pod-product-compliance
Lightning Source LLC
Chambersburg PA
CBHW071514150426
43191CB00009B/1524